The Venom and The Rose
Regina Bergen

Copyright © 2025 by Regina Bergen.

All rights reserved.

No portion of this book may be reproduced in any form without written permission from the publisher or author, except as permitted by U.S. copyright law.

For those who had to break before they could bloom;

For those who've been the venom *and* the rose;

For those who finally realized that their worth isn't measured by those who couldn't see it;

And for myself, who finally found the strength and courage to plant new gardens in the ashes of what burned.

May these pages remind each of you that your reflection belongs to you alone.

Final Words

I said goodbye to you again today.
So many words unsaid between us—
But, this time, I wouldn't let "I love you"
be among them, so I said it aloud
for the first time in our multi-year
history of being more than friends
but less than a couple.
-Lovers-
But only in secret, in hiding,
when and where no one else could see.
As I expected, you didn't say it back.
You said nothing at all, in fact,
and just watched me walk away.
But, then again, you'd always meant
more to me than I did to you.
The only thing worse than breaking up
is feeling the pain of a breakup
when there was nothing to even break.

Lesson

The most difficult lesson
I've learned from you and me,
is that you can't have someone
who doesn't want to be had.
You can't make another
love you if it's not in their nature,
or if you're just not enough.

Bitter

The outside air raps against my face,
cold for the first time in weeks,
even though it's mid-November.
The end to an Indian summer throws
a much harder punch without you.
In the past, we'd have been thinking
of frolicking in the snow and ice,
but it seems these days are different.
Now, nothing is icier than my glare
as I watch you trade me in for a
newer model—younger, less used up.
One not tainted by the pull of children
on her body, wallet, or years of trauma
on a delicate psyche, now stretched thin
by all the ways you told me I didn't matter.
We used to look forward to the first snow,
but now all I can think of is how the
fuck I'm going to get the driveway cleared.

Wise Up

You learn a lot when you're
the first of your friends
to get divorced...
Even the "good guys" are trash.
You're single now:
fair game, probably wounded.
So, what does it matter
whether they are or not?
Knowing how horrible
the ones you once trusted
as friends are when left to their
own devices makes it really
REALLY hard to date.
I can count the good ones
on just a few fingers...
Not even a full hand.
You should all be
ashamed of yourselves for
landing in one of my poems.

I Called Him "Boston"

I quasi-dated a guy in college
who now no longer exists...
Fine, I'm an open book—
we were good friends who
partied too much and couldn't
keep our hands off each other.
Still, to me, the loss is strange.
It has always stung on a deeper
level than I would have anticipated.
Not that any of this was expected.
Really, is it ever until it's too late?
I had always called him "Boston"
for the rather obvious reason
that it was where he came from—
with the 'ah' accent and all.
And he was one of the good guys.

Maybe he drank a little too much,
and partied harder than he should—
but it was college, you know?
The world was better off
with him in it, with his light on.
Even if we rarely talked by the time
he ceased his earthly form,
it was a comfort just to know
he existed on the same plane.
He would have been my age now.
Of course, he would have been—
we were the same age...
In fact, he was a little younger.
In my mind, now, he is eternally 19,
aging mentally paused by our abrupt
departure from each others' lives,
and later, by his sinking into soil.
Maybe he was supposed to
get married and have children of his own,
divorce, or even win big in the lottery.
Maybe we were meant to reconnect
to have a whirlwind second-chance
romance bloom out of nowhere,
somewhere deep in our 40's.
Maybe he was even my soulmate.
It's doubtful, but possible, right?
And with the way my life is going,
it would make sense that the
potential love of my life would
put a bullet in his head before

we even got things started.
But, listen to me... grasping at straws.
Look at how unhinged I've become:
crafting romances where none exist
because Romeo is already dead
and Juliet gave up trying ages ago.
If I could go back in time, I'd tell him
that country music isn't so bad—
that I was just an angry teen,
and there wasn't enough screaming
in it for me at that time of angst.
Maybe we could have listened to it
together, if he had held on a bit longer.
I'm sorry I wasn't there, Boston.
I'm sorry I didn't see any signs.
And I still think of you often.

Broken Wings

Remember when you bandaged
my broken wings, and promised
me that your repairs would hold?
That you'd take care of everything?
You lied, then you left me alone.
Crimes I'll never forgive nor forget,
left here crippled and unable to
fly free from this haunted place,
tied to each line on your face.
I can't erase you from my mind
because of the permanent scars
etched in the trauma of you walking
out the door in a pin-straight line.
No apologies, no looking back,
you left me wounded on the floor.

As Long as We're Happy

I don't need forever.
I don't want promises
that trickle too far into
the future, having learned
the hard way that trusting
uncertainty is dangerous,
treacherous turf to tread.
But I need to know it's
only me for you and
you for me until our end.
However long we are happy.
I don't expect it to be
THE end. Just ours.
But, in the time between,
the hours or days, perhaps
weeks, months or even years,

that we allow ourselves
to get lost in each other,
I don't want to share your heart.
Trust isn't something that
comes easily to me...
A privilege broken too
many times over already.
It is earned first, then lost.
And never granted freely.
Why is it so hard to be
simply one, the one, not
one amongst others?
I'm beginning to believe that
true love is a one-sided myth,
and the one who loves less
will always come out ahead.

H.S. Sweetheart

There are things I never said
back when we were young
and naive; new to all that
it meant to love and be loved
fully and faithfully in return.
I was so weak back then,
and my heart still jealous
because it hadn't yet
learned to trust yours.

How soon those lessons
were uncovered, then lost.
But I digress...

I never told you about how the
nights we spent in your old room,
the one at your parents' house,
enveloped in the softest sheets and
blankets in your bed that became ours,

probably saved my life several
hundred times over, maybe more.

In my greatest time of need,
amidst blinding, angsty sorrow,
a deep darkness enveloped my world.
You became the only light, my reason.
And through it all, you remained steadfast.
You held me, unflinching, unafraid of
my scars, offering true love and friendship-
And I'm certain I didn't make it easy.

...I still do that self-isolation thing
when my world gets too dark...
But I digress again.

We may not have lasted the test of time,
or held some deep, undying trust,
or even ignored every temptation,
but, still, I owe you my life for saving
the small slivers of sanity that remain
during those years when the world
tried it's hardest to rip them away;
when anger crept in, without warning,
over choices made out of necessity
that had too devastating of an impact
on my fragile, shaky little world.

Decisions that left me powerless,
a lost little girl in a brand-new body,

a new school, a whole new life.

As I struggled to remember
who I was and wanted to be,
you stayed. You waited.
You were mine and I was yours.
Without a second thought,
you gave me the gift of a family
that taught me what I needed
to learn in order to love my own—
out loud and proud, with
"I love you" every single day.

When I struggled to connect
with mine, you offered me yours.
You selflessly gave your love
and they, theirs, for free...
and you'll never know how many
times that saved me from losing
my internal battle with myself.

Things I Recall

Your room was my safe space.
Your legs fit behind mine like
puzzle pieces, perfectly curled
into a spoon-shaped embrace—
doing nothing but sleeping
(sometimes, anyway).

I remember your tissue pile.
You were allergic to everything,
but you'd never give up a pet.
Even your snoring was my comfort,
not unpleasant, despite its volume,
because it told me you were there.

We watched improv comedy shows
and let the outside world slip away
to the power of a science fiction series,
as we went on our own explorations
of each other, growing up together.

If those four walls could talk,
they'd tell a story about young love.
Two people with every freedom
to leave, but who chose to stay,
possibly for a bit too long.

Stay

You must stay
an arm's length
at all times
for safekeeping
of the parts of
me that remain.
My tears ran dry
a long time ago,
and I'm not about
to bust down a
fully functional dam.

Traumatized

I remember waking up
and thinking it was just
like any other day
until I went to swing my
legs off the bed and
found I couldn't move.
The colors of the rainbow
are beautiful until they
are painted across your skin,
each spot stinging more than
the ones that came before.
I stayed there all day,
lost somewhere between
excruciating pain and,
even worse, a numbness
that carved gaps into my
mind, excavating the places
where I would spend the
rest of my life hiding any

slivers of memory that
threatened my survival.
It was the day I learned
how to put the past behind
and move on, by pushing
it hard out of existence.
Burying it in the embers of
the fires you set within me.
It didn't happen.
None of this happened
because if it did, then
I can't go on living.
This may not be healing,
but it is how to get by
when living is too much.

Fairy Tales

You want what you want.
But me? I want the fairy tale.
I want the sappy love story,
with the happily ever after.
The one with two lead roles—
you and me, me and you.
Not you, me, her, and a few
others thrown in on the side,
unbeknownst to me, just
for kicks, for good measure.
I've tried to tone down my
jealous heart to hold onto
the ecstasy of your arms—
but it's a lost cause when
thinking of you with anyone
else sends me spiraling.
You can call it ethical
until you're blue in the face,
because you shun the words

'exclusive' and 'couple,'
but it doesn't make my heart
feel any less inept at the
having and holding part
when you're looking to
climb into bed with every
waitress who brings us food.

Fake

Sunlight fades into the dreaded night,
that grim time when reality crashes
headfirst into the world you've invented,
and the lines between who you are
and who you pretend to be are blurred.

Your truth is revealed from beneath the
mask you wear just to survive each day,
and you're terrified to let anyone stay
to see the you that you allow when no one
else is there to witness the innate darkness.

As it turns out, Miss Sunshine isn't always
a ray of light, and positivity gets old fast.

As nighttime falls, you keep on falling,
facing the violence of being struck
with the realization that you've been
living for something that no longer exists—

but you don't know how to leave it behind.

So, you wait out the night, refusing sleep
for fear that it will erase the threads of
what once was, the fibers you cling to
as if they're made from the last remaining
embers of magic in a world dull and defeated.

You stay awake to guard your spark,
to keep the fire alive that lets you face
another day and tend to the burns
left by countless hours of faking sunshine,
when you want to embrace the stars.

Reflections

When I look in the mirror,
I see scars no one else can.
Blatant, obvious, ugly.
Hideous and unconcealable
amidst the ordinary players,
like here-and-there freckles
and blemishes whose unsightly
presence I am equally aware of.
These wounds run deeper, though,
shrouded beneath the surface,
albeit impossible to ignore
as my reflection has become
one I no longer recognize.
I'm forced to search the profile
more deeply, to scour the image
staring back at me, with eyes
dimmer than they once were,
just to find pieces of myself.
The me I used to be is gone,

hiding behind all I've become
through all I've given up and
all that has given up on me.
Makeup can only go so far
when the past is fighting to
leave permanent reminders
on the lines of my face
and the depth of my eyes,
through the multitude of
secret tears that I've cried.

Means to an End

It's all done and over with,
strings cut, but never tied
up neatly with a pretty bow.
Sometimes I think about
whether or not he ever
thinks about me back.
If he's checked in on me,
or asked my old friends
how I've been or where I am.
Am I surviving or thriving?
I know he doesn't because
I was merely a means to
an end he reached long ago.
Still, I can't help but wonder.

A Strong(ish) Woman

She skirts the line between
faked confidence and that
damsel-in-distress vibe,
jumping from one side
to the other with ease.

It all depends on the mood,
sometimes changing by the hour!

She's not the type to ask for help,
but willing to accept a trade,
so she's constantly giving herself away
hoping for something of value in return.

Lost

I wrote the most incredible
poem in the car today.
It was profound and perfect,
but it only existed in my head.

I lost it somewhere between
here and there, so now all I have
are these meandering verses
about misplacing my own words.

PTSD

Holy f*ck.
Who knew
you could
experience
PTSD
symptoms
simply by
driving past
your ex-hookup-
turned-heartbreak's
apartment
when it's
unavoidably
smack dab
in the middle
of the only
real route to
somewhere
unavoidable.

But here we are...
Shaking, gasping,
sitting in the car.

Forty-One Changes Everything

I hid things for 40 years
and it got me nowhere,
left me with nothing.
Nothing ventured,
nothing gained.
So, now I'm all in.
It's all fair game.
In this moment of
self-revelation,
self-preservation,
I'm here tearing off
band-aids and screaming
secrets I once thought
were better left unsaid.
Throwing threats under
the bus and refusing

to keep it all quiet.
You can keep your
hush money, too.
I'll hold my humiliation
out for anyone who
wants a chance to
take a stab at it...
I've reached the point
where I no longer care
enough to collapse
under the weight of
your unjust judgments
without a fair trial.

Someday

Someday, somehow,
you'll be the first
to reach out.
Just not today.

Flight Risk

The world spins differently
when you move through life
each day wanting something
so badly you're willing to
fool yourself into making the
same mistakes again and again,
expecting it to end differently.
It becomes an endless cycle
of hope, haze, headache,
And finally... heartbreak.
- Lather, rinse, repeat -
You search, but never find,
love but are never loved,
and pass up perfectly acceptable
options under the guise that
it just wasn't meant to be...
The chemistry wasn't right,
But maybe it's really about you.
Maybe you refuse to let it be.

Closed off to anything new,
always reaching for the past,
how many times have you walked
away when you were meant to stay?

Different

I'm so deeply flawed in form
and the ability to function
in ways deemed proper and
acceptable to a world
so painfully misaligned with
all I want to be and offer.
But, even so different
from those around me,
I want to be seen, heard,
noticed by the people in it.
To come out of the shadows
from time to time just
to remind myself that while
I may be composed of a
different substance and
structured in ways they'll
never, ever understand,
I am still of this Earth.
And I still matter.

Prey

You play games.
A wolf in sheep's clothing.
You, predator.
Me, the prey.
Or am I?
You think you
have me fooled,
but you don't.
I'm not nearly as
dumb as you
make me out to be
from up high on
your pedestal,
gazing down and
seeing only tiny
slivers of who I am.
You're an excellent actor,
but I've done theater
for my entire life.

I can fake it just as well,
if not better. Actually,
probably much better.
Sometimes, my decisions
are based on how I want
things to be rather than
how they really are.
So, I make them, knowing
full well that severing the ties
that bind me to you only
becomes a later problem.

Rejected

Why is it that he looks
SO FUCKING CUTE
only after I decided I
didn't want him?!
God, I'm so fucked up.

The Habit of Humor

I wear my scars differently
than the others you've met.
In fact, you'd never even
know that they're there
(until I point it out in a poem).
Hiding behind a steadfast
wall of self-depricating humor,
fueled by wit and sarcasm,
I can ward off those who
would otherwise judge.
Instead of weird, I'm funny,
transforming my deepest
struggles into comedy gold.
You won't be so quick to
brush me aside if I can
still strike a chord that draws
that crooked smile horizontally
across the lines of your face.
It's such a beautiful smile,

after all, even though
we are only just friends.

Child

Stubborn child,
you were once
known for your
fiery temper;
flipping tables
over unintended
outcomes of a
Monopoly game
gone awry.
Now, you keep
your feelings
buried, shrouded,
down deep
beneath a
thick veil of
secrets and
silence.
Bottled up
and corked,

until the next
time you lose
your grip and
lose control.
The breakdown
is all too imminent
Didn't you know?
There's beauty
in the breakdown,
sanity in the
shredding of
your strength.
Power in finally
falling to your knees.
And this is when
things will finally start to
change for you...
If you only let them.

Snapped

I need a break.
I can feel my sanity
slipping away.
Just like before.
Just like it did
in the days when
it was me and you,
but really only me.
Me, alone, on my own.
On call 24/7.
No relief in sight.
Even when you were
here, you weren't.
Glued to your phone,
and your indiscretions,
and to your unwavering
commitment to break
me down to nothing.
Babies, kids, dogs.

THE VENOM AND THE ROSE

Wants, needs, messes.
An entire household
set on one person,
watching the other 'rest.'
When you left, I thrived.
First breaks in a decade
to remember who I was.
It brought reprieve.
Moments of quiet.
Opportunities for peace.
I need a break again.
Not your idea of
the type of break
that I deserved...
Enough time to go to
the pharmacy,
or to run errands,
or grocery shop,
or do laundry,
or take a kid,
or pick them up.
In returning to
this house with the
ones who came after,
and keeping up with
your old ways,
you've taken my sanity.
And this time, it's worse...
We aren't even together!

Run

Listen, and listen well...
If he threatens you with leaving,
then he's already left.
If he says it will be over,
then, it already is.
He's already gone.
Run. Don't look back.
You are worth so much
more than what he will
ever be able to give you.
Trust me on this one.

Girl

Thick skin, thick thighs.
Pretty emerald
green eyes.
Solid heart.
Solid soul.
Psyche only
half, not whole.
Broken before.
Broken again.
Always chooses
red flag men.
Fakes her smile.
Fakes her armor.
Walls built high
to hide her trauma.
Today, she's brave.
Today, she's funny.
But when she's alone,
she's far from sunny.

Sins

Skin on skin and
mouth to mouth,
our bad decisions
flow like cheap wine.
You taste like lust,
and beautiful mistakes.
But you smell like the
smoke clogging my mind,
clouding my judgment.
By now, I know better than
to believe a word you say,
but still, I let you inside,
pretending that it's love
or something like it.
Past transgressions are left
in the past; neither forgiven
nor forgotten, simply ignored
in the heat of these moments.
But these sins come at a cost,

a hefty price tag that I keep
paying just for the chance at
passing another night in the
ecstasy of your arms.

Here

Here, we bleed in black and white.
Words on paper shed from places
deep within, from parts of ourselves
we usually hide, shield from the light.
Here, we trade bare skin, information,
and booze to escape the thoughts
that would otherwise haunt us through
the darkest parts of the lonely nights.
Here, we bleed from gaping wounds,
some seen and others kept secret,
and we never once ask for a bandage.
We know we travel this road alone.
Here, we are merely who we are,
but never even close to who others
want us to be, think we are, or
believe we are meant to behave.
Here, we are not who they wanted
us to become back when we were kids.
We've tossed our potential out through

tiny cracks in those same windows we
once used to sneak out of the house.
Here, our past lends itself to our future.
He hurt me back then, so I'll hurt the
other ones before they get a chance:
A perfect plan, until it backfires.
Here, sifting through a trove of
different deceptions becomes the
norm for all of us, our daily bread,
a penance for our poor choices in love.
It is here that we fall victim to a
tragic metamorphosis from all that
we once were and all we could have been,
to the disappointing reality of what is left
after life has sucked out all our kindness,
and killed our compassion, leaving
hollow shells of the people we were before,
and no room for what-could-have-been.

Bring the Light

Feed off the light and
let the darkness fall away.
Become so much more
than the masses who
are still just struggling
to be seen in a world
they don't understand.
Come bearing your kindness
and compassion in full force,
without apologies, without shame,
and offer it up freely to others.
There can be no cost set upon
such gifts as these, for they
will multiply upon themselves
when given without provisons.
Put the past behind you to allow
the movement toward your future
with a heart open and ready for
whatever fate has in store.

Leaving behind the anger from
mistakes made in your yesterdays
is the only way to grant freedom
from trauma blocking your tomorrows.
Be the kindness. Be the change.
Unbind the broken from their chains.

Glimmer

It's when almost all hope is lost
that the glimmer of possibility
slips in silently from the sidelines.
It creeps in without any fanfare,
making it easier to go unmentioned
if things don't work out... again.
Still, the signs are all there:
Laughter over coffee at the
diner where we first met,
a kiss shared in the rain,
just like the first time.
This time, it lingered too long
and made me miss my meeting.
We've tried this before, I know.
Maybe it's time to try again.

Shh...

Shh...
We don't keep secrets here.
We trade them for whatever
gets us through another day,
or another night, or even
just the next moment.

Starved for attention,
you sell your most private
truths to the highest bidder...
To have, to hold, to judge,
or to tell the world.

Numb

Sometimes, I think I keep
going back to you just to
remember how to cry.
I've been numb so long,
and you're the only one
who knows my heart
enough to crush it
without even trying.
When the salty tears
stream down my face,
everything I've kept
bottled up for so long
rushes out all at once,
cleansing me of sorrows
I've kept clenched inside,
waiting for the right time
to let them into the world.
It's a wound you inflicted,
but one born of self-sabotage.

Too large for a band-aid,
but not quite as lethal
as the bullet holes your
words could once cause
(before I put on my armor.)
Now I never take it off,
and I've become harder,
stronger, but more broken,
from having met you.

Hole

Here I go again.
Down the rabbit
hole that is you.
Deeper each time
until there's nothing
left of me to give.
Each ending is the
very last time... I swear.
Until it isn't, anymore.
Until it starts again.
I know I promised it was
over after the last bit of us,
but your words are drugs
that pierce through
these layers of skin,
too thin from all you've
already taken away.
How many times can
one person make the

same exact mistake?
How many times can
I do this to myself
before I fall in too deep
to reel it all back in?
How much longer
before this goes too far?
Before I lose the will
to come back at all.

The Venom & the Rose

She's the venom and the rose,
too soft to withstand the storm,
but she'll make her mark when
you turn to leave her behind.

Deep punctures you never even
saw coming, and they'll eat at you
until you realize all you gave up,
leaving festering wounds in their wake.

Wounds, like mine, that don't heal.
You'll miss her when you realize
the price you paid to have your
cake and eat another on the side.

You see what I did there?
I hope it was all worth it in the end.
And it's funny... well, maybe that's
not the right word, but I digress...

Spoiler alert:
As it turns out, 'she' is me, and it's
only "funny" how you didn't think
I'd see the truth hiding in the grass.

Darling, I knew it all along, but denial
is more than just a river in Egypt.
Snakes like you don't ever change,
they simply shed their skin and try again.

They start over with someone else
when their secrets are discovered,
becoming a new version of themselves
once their sins are uncovered.

You'll live in regret, but I'll get by,
because I can be the venom or
the rose, the pinprick or the petals.
You simply slither in, strike, then leave.

You take everything that you want,
and give nothing in return.

Faker

She fakes it 'til she makes it,
'til her plastic smile stays glued,
permanent, like the lines
deepening on her face
as youth fades without
even a whispered goodbye,
without a backward glance,
leaving no trace behind.

She's always been an actress,
but now she's on her own again,
and she needs the attention
as she tries to hold something,
anything that she can grasp to
regain her footing, her composure.

Her head held high in a perfect
display of counterfeit confidence,
her world spins out of control.

She knows there's no fix for a life
that doesn't feel like it's hers anymore.
How could it be? How could this be?

So, she lets it all go, choosing a
free fall into nothingness, no 'chute.
Not even a whispered cry for help.
She's been faking it for so long that
no one would hear it, anyway.

His

My voice hitches in my throat
as your hand catches on my hip,
holding me in place through a
wordless declaration of the things
you know that I already know...
"Mine," it says in no uncertain terms,
a silent announcement of your
ownership of what is, what was,
and all that will be between us.
I don't fight the unfair terms anymore:
I'm yours, but you belong to no one.
It isn't worth the time or effort,
knowing that I won't leave you
behind if it means being alone.
Your words still make me smile,
even if you're saying those same
things to so many others who still
think they're the only ones...
At least I know the truth,

but I'm in this too deep to
walk away from it now.

The Reasons Why

She hates her smile,
says it gives her
chipmunk cheeks,
and makes her flaws
all the more obvious.
He says it's beautiful,
and lights up the dark.
Her own body is her
breaking point,
a trigger for tears
like none other.
But, he makes
her feel pretty
just the way she is:
Thick thighs
and pretty eyes.
She's damaged goods,
and she knows it.
Broken beyond repair,

but he doesn't ever
seem to care.
Even when she dives
in deep, full force,
invited but unrequited,
then runs away
when it feels like
a heartbreak just
waiting to happen.
He's still there,
ready for the cycle
to start again, revisited.
Maybe not 'waiting,'
in a cinematic sense,
but always there,
just the same.
It's far from a fairytale.
There's no happily ever
after to be had,
but he's still there.
Maybe it's just a
temporary remedy for
her loneliness, but...
Doesn't his continuing
presence through
all of her bullshit
count for something?

Raging

You want truth? You once told me:
"Always speak your truth," after all...
Poetic bullshit from someone who
spews lies like it's part of breathing.
Fine. I'm angry enough to dish it out.
Finally... It took me long enough!
Step back because tonight my words
are going to pierce like weapons,
and your armor is a fucking joke;
cloth, spray painted to look like steel.
Weak, just like you, frail and phony.
You can take the fake ass smile
I've been plastering across my face
for years and shove it up your ass.
I'm sick of trying to sparkle in your skies.
You don't want stars; you want a meteor!
Someone to hurl themselves to the Earth
and explode in a fireball of destruction
while you look on, wide-eyed, shaking

your head: "She was always a little crazy."
And it's all for your approval, your praise.
I've been that girl for too long and, now,
I'm going to burn up in your skies in a
breathtaking display of defiance,
but I'll never hit the ground at your feet
because I am not yours. Never was.
Never will be (you've made that clear).
For a long time, I believed it was me.
All along, me. That I wasn't enough.
Not pretty enough. Not thin enough.
Not deep enough. Not smart enough.
You made me feel like I was only
good enough to be a toy, no more.
When, in reality, it was you who lacked
the magic to let something truly unfold.
You let fear control your life, masking it
and calling it "strength" and "resilience,"
and, for that, I hope someday you
wonder whether we could have been
more than you ever let us become.

Your Room

Bleeding false promises from your lips
without saying a word, you press them
against mine, firm, much too firm for love.
This isn't where people go to fall for
one another, merely a place to
forget the ones who came before
and left scars of trauma in their wake.
We hide out here – together – but never
really "together," seeking the comfort
of another body to warm the long,
lonely nights and ease the deep chill.
We find temporary solace in two souls
that will never commit to one another.
Apparently, exclusivity is a dirty word
when you're in your forties and single.
After all, who would want just one
when there's so much fun to be had
with just a few exchanges of text and
several kind words to build trust?

I mean... I would...
But, Lord, I can't say that out loud.
Not here. Not with you.
Those are the types of thoughts that
get internally censored for fear of
winding up sleeping in my own bed.
The horror of being alone far outweighs
that of being yours for only the nights
when nothing better comes along.
It's fine. I'm fine. All of this is fine.
But, "love" or "us" is entirely off the table
and out of the question.

Cold

I forgot to warm my car up this morning,
and my ice scraper disappeared.
I was already having a crap day,
and the last thing I needed was to sit
in the cold waiting for the defrosters to
kick in to give me vision while the tears
that fell became frozen to my face.
...But...
It's just another day living the dream.

Unbelievable

I don't believe in
magic anymore.
That's it.
That's the poem.

Sick Cycle

Moving on doesn't come easily for me,
even when it's to get away from
something that was never real
in the first place, merely a convenience.
Sometimes, I wonder which of my sins
I am still punishing myself for,
whether it was ever my sins at all.
What could make me hate myself
so much that it keeps me stuck,
seeking atonement in a cycle of
self-sabotage so strong that all
attempts to break free are futile?
He can't possibly care about me,
because if he did, he wouldn't let me
keep coming back to this circle of hell.
My eyes hold the shame of someone
who has tried to run so many times,
only to return, begging for breadcrumbs.
If only my therapist could see me now...

So much for her success story, right?
So strong. So healed. Yeah, right.
I threw that out the window at the
first chance I saw to lay in your arms.

Lost

Where do you go when
your world is falling apart,
and everyone you used to
run to is either long ago
disappeared or dead?
I guess you just stay lost.

Masked

"You always seem so happy!"
"I love your bubbly personality!"
"You're not shy at all!"
"You're such an open book,
...It's so refreshing!"
These are the words they say now,
and the ones I hear, but they
certainly aren't grounded in truth.
If this is the me you see,
then you're not in my inner circle
(but don't worry, no one is).
I learned from a very early age
about the masks I'd have to wear
to fit in with the others.
I know how to play nice with
the other kids in the sandbox,
even after they've stolen and
read my diary aloud to the
entire class, or tortured me

shamelessly at the slumber party,
or forced secrets from my lips
under guises of false friendships,
only, later, to reveal them to our world.
These were once the connections
I so desperately yearned for, sought.
I've seen what feeling threatened
by the new girl can do to a clique
of middle school girls who aren't
prepared to fall face first from their
precious, precarious little pedestals
without a dirty fight that I was
nowhere near prepared for.
I barely had the strength to wake up,
get up, and put one foot in front
of the other to make it out the door,
let alone grasp at trophies that
I never even wanted in the first place,
as my whole world was crumbling.
Still, I knew how to pretend everything
was fine in my long-sleeves and stacked
bracelets - always up with the latest styles
(or something like that, right?)
Remember the year I finally went dark?
The year that I quit volleyball?
Then softball? Then theater?
It's really all a blur to me now, and
sometimes I'm not sure which parts
are even real and which I've made up
to fill the trauma gaps that fell in line

THE VENOM AND THE ROSE

with the rest of my life falling to pieces...
Either way, in a series of moments,
I threw it all away, everything I had
worked for, and it made no sense
to anyone in my world how I could choose
to fade away from the scrutinizing eyes
of the fakes and the phonies,
and choose to be entirely alone.
But, in those moments, I chose kindness
over the cruelty of the entire system,
even if it was my downfall in many ways.
Hindsight is twenty-twenty, you know?
Go ahead and act like you know where
I come from and what I've been through.
It matters very little, ultimately.
You'll never know my secret battles
hidden well by a re-written history,
strategically shrouded in a carefully
constructed web of my own protective armor.
Just as I'll never, ever know the real you
and all the things it took to make you
who you have now become in 2025.

Sick

These fever poems are potent.
The past seems too close,
the future too far, and the
present doesn't even exist at all.
Lost somewhere between here
or there, it fades out into nothing,
leaving me cradled only by what
came before and what is yet
to come, stranded but safe,
blanketed in the knowledge that
I'm still in the company of myself.
But the visions shift as my
temperature rises, catching 102.
And the room is too cold,
but my body is too hot.
The finger pointers I'd tried,
for all these years, to erase,
return in a taunting parade,
spinning webs of questions

and self-doubt, strangling me
with long-dead accusations
of things I never did with people
who I never even knew...
It wasn't me, I promised you.
But my word was never enough,
so in my most trying times
I'm still haunted by the ghosts
of those who took you away
with false reports of betrayal.
Not me. Not once. Not ever.

Season's Greetings

"You haven't been happy lately,"
they begin to tell me in December,
amidst the flurries of snow and
played out greetings of the season.
"Thanks for noticing, finally,"
is how I want to respond,
but we all know I can only be rude
in my books and poems,
so, I only smile and tilt my head.
"It's been a hard year," I manage,
leaving out the previous three to five,
and it buys me enough time to
construct a better response to the
next inquiry into my wellbeing
from someone who really couldn't
care less about the answer.

Repeat

I fall back into your arms
with just a single gaze and
a few doting messages to
calm my racing thoughts
about how we will never work.
You do nothing further to
assure me that we will,
but even so, the dopamine
rush of being back in your
thoughts, however temporarily,
is enough to bring me back
... at least for the night.

Redundant

And here we are, back again,
straddling that line between
losing our hearts or falling apart.
Maybe the hundredth time will
be the charm for us, right?
I pretend it's possible, if only
to make myself feel better
about the whole damn thing...
We have to be getting close to
100 by now; don't you think?
Or, maybe it just feels that way
because it's so redundant.
Your heart has never been mine,
but every so often there are
glimpses past it's high walls,
and I can guess what it'd be like
if you ever truly let me inside.
But, guessing is a gamble,
and I'm not good at counting cards,

so I merely accept what we are
until the next time I come unglued,
Text blocks dished out all around
that we both know won't last.

Dopamine

Dopamine is ruining my life.
Your inconsistency is the only
thing that is ever consistent,
and it's feeding a toxic addiction.
Dopamine. Oxytocin.
Cortisol. Adrenaline.
These little jolts here and there,
with nothing in between,
keep me coming back for more,
draining the ability to function
from my executive functioning!
I know how all of this works to
some extent... but I'm not quite
prepared to give up the highs—
even if it all amounts to only
breadcrumbs, and being one
of many women you refer to
as your "close friends."

Sometimes

She's seeking her path,
lost amidst all the stop signs
and one-way streets.

She carries on because
giving up wasn't ever an option,
and she's come too far for that.

Even though it sometimes feels
like she's moving in circles,
at least she is still moving.

Each forward footfall brings
her one step closer to the place
where she was meant to be.

Each wrong turn leads her right,
if only by process of elimination,
to the things meant for her.

Still, sometimes, she loses her place
in a world spinning too fast
for her to cling to any safety net.

Sometimes, she falls and is left
brushing dirt off with unclean hands.
She has spent a lifetime just trying
to be good, but sometimes, she gets lost.

Crossroads

You can't love me the way
that I need you to—
and I can't pass another day
feeling like I'm not enough
for your whole heart.
So, it ends here and now
at the crossroads between
all that was once between us
and nothing, going forward.
But, this time, we will both
turn and walk away in peace,
leaving a kiss on the wind.
Calm, collected, without rage.
This time, it isn't about
the bitterness or the past,
but the acceptance that
we just aren't meant to be
more than we are already,
and false hope has been

a barrier to finding what
I've been seeking all along.
You don't have the heart to
love me the way I deserve,
and I'm beginning to realize
that it's all for the best.

Career Goals

Extra! Extra!
Read all about it!
Young girl, wait, no...
(she nearly forgets she's
no longer a card-carrying
member of the youth
of the nation, and it robs
her of another easy excuse
for her shoddy decision-making
and piss-poor judgment.)
...I digress...
Extra! Extra!
Read all about it!
Forty-plus mom falls from a
self-constructed pedestal of
'fake it 'til you make it,'
breaks heart on impact,
then misses out on two months
of writing she should have

been pushing out on the daily.
Newsflash! Get it here first!
The grind comes full stop,
and her story is smeared
across the front page
(of her Facebook, that is!)
Gasp By who, you ask?
Well, by herself, of course.
When you're still faking it,
and haven't quite made it yet,
no one cares enough to
talk about you behind your back.
That's the trick, you know?
Mind the jealousy.
That's when you know you've
finally hit the big time...
When the talkers start to talk,
and the posters start to post.
Then, you're well on your way
to achieving your dreams.

Trauma

Sure, she's beautiful,
but, Lord, the trauma
runs deep in that one!
She hides it like an expert
in the art of deception,
keeping herself always an
arm's reach away from
anyone who tries to get
close enough to cause
her to drop her guard.

Tough Love

Moon on high.
No alibi for
where I've been
or what I've done.

It's okay.
I'm willing
to go down for
my transgressions.

He is fire.
And I'm not
prepared to walk
away from this heat.

I am water.
I turn to vapor
in his presence and
forget to contain myself.

I emerge.
Condensed, I am
all the things I swore
that I'd never allow again.

I'm lesser now.
Shallower than when
this whole thing began,
weaker knowing that
us two will never become one.

Left Behind

This is the last poem
I will write about you.
Your gestures are far
from grand, barely there.
Still, I will always cling
to the hope that one day
you'll bypass my blocks
to get me one message:
'You made a mistake.'
Just so I can walk away,
and leave you standing there
with your jaw dropped
and your eyes wide in shock
at the knowledge that
I've finally washed my hands
of you and left the past
behind me, where it belongs.
That's right - you belong
behind me where you can't

get in my way again.

Let Yourself

Let yourself choose
the one you've been
hiding from out of
the deep-seated fear
that things could
actually work out.

Let yourself pick
the possibility of
peace over Mr. Morally
Gray; a non-committal
volcano waiting
to erupt and launch
you from his world.

Choose the one
who doesn't need
you to change him
into what is best

for your heart
and your soul.

Choose him this time—
the same one who
was always there,
just waiting for you
to come to your senses
and give him a shot.

It's time to do
something kind
for yourself.
It's time to stop
the self-sabotage,
and let yourself be
HAPPY.

Stagnant

I arise daily to alarms,
ear-piercing and rough
(Yes, it takes several),
and breakfast thrown
together with a callous
disregard for the
importance of starting
the day on the right foot.
Caffeine—strong & black.
There's no room for
light or sweet in a world
that feels so cold as of late.
So, I settle for scalding—
at least it feels real.
Moments blur and,
suddenly, the day ends
before it even had a chance
to get itself started.
I'm no further ahead

than I had been before.
Last week, last month,
or even last year.
Stagnant, I wait here
for something, anything,
a sign of hope or one
saying the end is near—
a dove of peace
or a bird of prey.
It's really all the same.
But no news comes
and the waiting game
feels as if it has gone
on for far too long.
Time ticks the moments
of my life away into a barrel
like fish, trapped enmasse.
And I shoot at them,
one by one, not out of
necessity but sheer boredom.
When does the good part
of this life finally start?
Or did I miss out on it during
that massive downward
spiral a few weeks ago?
Or the ones that came before?

Unrequited

My love, as it turns out,
is also thicker than water.
So viscous that when
I tried to remove it from
your grip, your clutches,
to bleed it from my veins,
still, it stayed behind.
It pooled beneath my skin,
leaving painful bruises,
invisible from the surface,
but draining my will from within.
I still choke on all the things
I pretended that you were,
(a person who never was)
and memories of someone
who didn't even exist.
I'm not proud of the way
I held on to all that we weren't
for so long; far too long.

It leaves me longing for
all of the nights wasted
on petty, one-sided hopes
and foolish fairytale dreams.
It leaves me reeling,
as if I'm still wandering amidst
your maze of mixed signals.

Poet

Dig deeper, your words are
not getting the attention
that they used to garner.
Cyclical, repetitive, and empty,
just like your thoughts.
Shock value fades when
it's always the same, you know?
But, you write for yourself,
not them, right?
At least you used to.

Committed

The hypocrisy of my incessant
complaints about red-flag men
with deep-seated fears of
commitment in any form
doesn't escape me one bit.
I'm just as bad as they are.
Worse, I'd be willing to bet.
At least they know what they want,
and some are even honest,
whereas I go spouting off
desires for "something more,"
"something real," and "more than this,"
then take off running every time
the opportunity presents itself.
You know what they say about
the definition of insanity, right?
Forget commitment...
I should probably be committed.

How Long?

How long does it take to fall
out of love with someone
you never should have
loved in the first place?

How long to untangle
the threads of memory
from around a heart that
should have known better?

How long will the days
spiral like autumn leaves,
each carrying a fragment
of what we almost were?

How long before I accept that
wisdom and want are strangers
passing in the night and
never the two shall meet?

How many phases of the moon
must I count, always wondering
when your name will stop tasting
like sugar and regret on my tongue?

Perhaps healing isn't measured
in hours or even heartbeats,
but in the slow acceptance
that some lessons can be learned
only by breaking our own rules.

And maybe the time it takes
to fall out of love is exactly
the same amount it will take
to forgive ourselves for
falling in the first place.

Failure

Papers strewn across the room,
I tried to write the perfect poem...
But I got lost somewhere between
the words I wanted to say and
the ones I thought you would
want to see written across the page.
Now, it seems we're at an impasse,
and this is all I have to show for it.

A Fairytale (This is Why I'm Single)

He will come with palms wide,
not clenched, except when our
fingers are threaded into
one another's, clinging tightly,
as he braves the wilderness of
both my written and still
unrevealed stories, my
secrets awaiting their light.
He will rise to meet me
on equal ground, the place
where we accept each other
for all that we are, and ask
for nothing more than that.
He will neither judge my past
nor shy from the prospect of
our future, harboring no fear

in his eyes when my poems reveal

my sharp edges,

open wounds,

and thundering silences.

He will read to me at night,

long into the overnight hours,

to calm the demons that strike

when the darkness falls,

his voice shushing me, not to

quiet my own but to bring peace.

Dominant, not through force,

but by his very presence,

I'll know I'm safe in his arms.

Arms that stay faithful,

not as a forced promise,

but as a living breath,

something desired, not insisted:

Love simply for the sake of love.

Depth for the sake of depth.

He will prove honest enough

to carry both the darkness and light,

that I harbor within my heart,

and to move through past shadows

without ever becoming them.

He will exist not to complete me,

but, instead, to walk through this life

by my side for however long

we may keep our happiness intact.

The Hardest Lessons

My most harrowing storms are
still shaped like your ghost,
haunting me as I move through
the rooms we used to frequent
back when we couldn't keep
our hands off each other.
I hear your whispers in the
smallest, most trivial things—
an extra glance toward my driveway,
thinking I may have heard your car,
or the phantom indent of your shape
in the places you most liked to sit.
Life, now, has become about learning
the hard lessons—the ones with
the power to shock and awe,
leaving us stunned and shell-shocked.
They bend and break us into pieces,
shards that make up a whole
that is smarter, wisened, but

harder, thicker-skinned, and jaded.
Love is no longer measured by its depth,
but by the strength it takes to let it go.
By how hard it is to dance with shadows
in now-empty spaces and seek solace
within the hollow places where
your laughter used to live and breathe.
They say time heals all wounds,
but leave out the part about how it
first breaks you open to start anew.
But you must learn the lessons.
Lessons like how to breathe again,
how to hold back the tears,
and how to rebuild your world
around the shape of someone's
absence instead of their presence—
a hole that will never be filled,
a space that once housed a heart
that was never yours to keep.
You must learn to take all of the
unsaid words, untouched caresses,
and unlived moments together,
and let them all go with the wind.
Release them like paper lanterns,
floating into the night to become
stars illuminating someone else's sky.
And in the surrender of one lover
to this inescapable fate, this agony,
there comes a new kind of love born:
A gentle acceptance that what

once was can no longer be,
a moment when the present is pushed
to the past, and you give into the unknown,
bowing and exiting the stage with poise,
with grace, and leaving the curtain ready,
and the spotlight on for what comes next.

Heavy

I carry your words like pebbles
housed, hidden, in my pocket,
tiny stones I never asked to hold.
Yet, still, they weigh me down.
Annoyed at their very presence,
angrier that I allow them to stay,
I pretend they don't exist.
But they press hard against my body,
leaving subtle bruises as I move
through the motions of this life,
shielding others from similar fates.
Why do I shelter them still when
I should scatter them in the dirt
to face the elements alone?
But, no, that's not in my nature.
So, I carry your words, his words, hers—
a multitude of accusations and
indications that I'll never be enough—
through the days, stacking them

into walls that fail me right when
I need them the most, those
moments of weakness, paralysis.
I see what I don't want to be in
those words, and perhaps I was
moving in the direction of
becoming something I'm not.
Even unwanted mirrors can show
us the reflections we need to see,
teaching us where we're still tender,
where we're still striving to be strong.
So, I allow myself to feel their weight
fully and intentionally, with as
much grace as I can muster,
before opening my pocket to the breeze
and watching them tumble free...
not because they didn't hurt,
but because I choose what burdens
to keep and to release from my life.

Half-Love

There's something inherently cruel
about this half-love I've finally
turned my heart away from.
A profound sting in the way it
lingers seductively in my doorway,
neither fully entering nor leaving,
like a morning fog that won't quite lift,
beckoning me back to get lost
in the wanting and the hoping
for the things that weren't ever ours.

You offered me pieces of yourself,
but scattered them like breadcrumbs,
always just enough to keep me
following the path to your door.
Master of charm, and then avoid;
you called it your villain era,
as if giving it a fancy name made it
somehow okay to teach me

that love shouldn't feel like waiting.

Remember how I used to swoon
for your midnight messages?
Now they're just ghosts in my phone,
haunting the person I used to be.
Some nights I still yearn for you
in the dark space before dreaming
sets in and delivers me to safety.
They say time heals all wounds,
but acceptance of what we are,
what we were, and what we never
would have been works faster:
the truth that I deserve more
than to be nothing more than
someone's maybe or almost.

Panic at the Laundromat

I know no one can see
the panic set in hard,
hidden behind years
of practice at masking
it behind my smile,
but the truth is that
I'm freaking out.
I can barely breathe
as I stand here
unloading a dryer
above another that
someone else wants
to access in what
seems like a hurry.

A simple act suddenly
becomes terrifying.

I'm moving as fast

as I can to unload
but the clothing tangles
into a clump that
becomes difficult to
remove from the dryer
and shove into my bag.
A sock falls to the floor
and the woman behind
me rolls her eyes.
(Maybe she didn't,
perhaps I imagined it.)
I lean down and pick it up.
Wait, is my sweatshirt
still covering my whole ass?
...I don't like how I look
in these pants...
Are people watching me?
(I know they aren't.)
They must think I'm
such a disaster.

God, how could I drop
so many articles of clothing?
This isn't rocket science!

I feel the room closing in
smaller, tighter, cramped.
And all eyes are on me.
(But they're probably not.)
I am painfully aware

that it's all in my head.
Still, that does nothing
to calm my racing thoughts.
FINALLY, the last pile!
There weren't this many
people when I came in here,
were there? I don't know.
Does everyone do their
laundry on Monday afternoon?
I'll have to make a note of that.

I don't usually come here for this
But my own dryer is broken.

I try to appear nonchalant,
as I take my laundry and
escape through the exit,
successfully out of peril
(at least as far as my
nervous system is concerned.)
It's rare that this type
of thing occurs anymore,
thanks to modern medicine,
but when it does, the feelings
of fear linger for hours after.
I am "safe" at my car now,
and I thank my lucky stars
I'm never too anxious
(anymore) to drive a car,
at the very least.

About the Author

Regina Bergen lives with her three children and two rescue dogs in the beautiful Hudson Valley region of New York. She has a B.A. in Environmental Studies and Latin American Studies and a Master's in Public Administration from Pace University.

Before writing and editing full-time, Regina worked as a fundraiser at a global environmental conservation organization and spent several years as a stay-at-home mom. She loves the outdoors, animals, cooking, coffee, and spending her free time with her kids and pets.

Social Media – Get in Touch!

Facebook, TikTok, Instagram, Goodreads:
ReginaBergenAuthor
www.ReginaBergen.com
WritingbyRegina@gmail.com

www.ingramcontent.com/pod-product-compliance
Lightning Source LLC
LaVergne TN
LVHW041227080426
835508LV00011B/1105